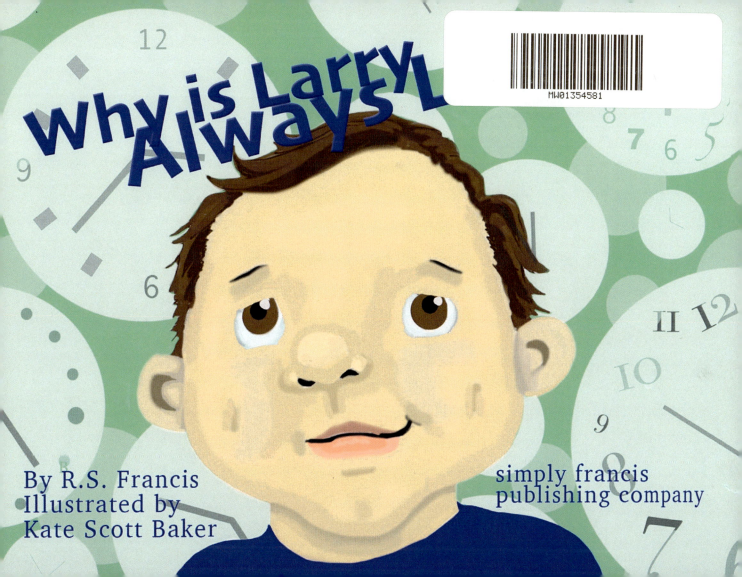

Copyright © 2020 by R.S. Francis and Kate E. Baker. All Rights Reserved.
Library of Congress Control Number:
ISBN: 978-1-63062-028-8 (paperback)
ISBN: 978-1-63062-029-5 (ebook)
Printed in the United States of America

simply francis publishing company
P.O. Box 329, Wrightsville Beach, NC 28480
www.simplyfrancispublishing.com
simplyfrancispublishing@gmail.com

Author's Dedication

This book is dedicated to my husband Larry. Thank you for teaching me that the journey is just as important as the destination and for always keeping me on my toes…after all, we wouldn't know what to do with a dull moment.

R.S. Francis is a certified Special Education (K-12) and General Education (K-6) teacher. She taught special education for 17 years across all grade levels (Pre-K-age 21) and continues to work in the elementary school setting. R.S. was born and raised in Youngstown, OH. She currently resides in Wilmington, NC with her husband Larry and their dog Josephine (Joey). Becoming a children's book author is a lifelong dream come true.

Author: R. S. Francis

Illustrator: Kate Scott Baker

Kate Scott Baker is a photographer and portrait painter. She has managed portrait studios in Pennsylvania and California and has taught preschool. Kate was born and raised in Sharon, PA and received her bachelor of fine arts degree from The Pennsylvania State University. She now lives in Warren, OH with her Husband Cory and dog Gunny. She had a wonderful time illustrating her first children's book and working with her beloved cousin, Rebecca.

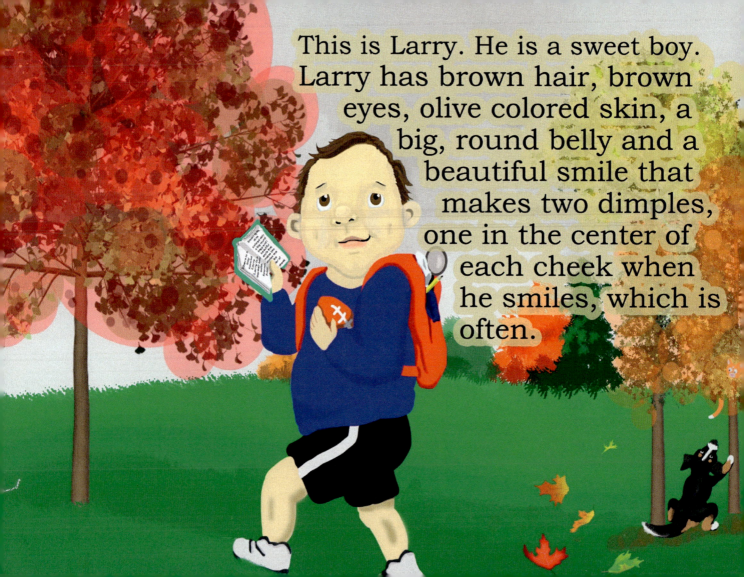

Larry lives in Sharon, Pennsylvania with his Mom, Dad, one brother and three sisters.

He is the oldest child and is always busy helping his younger siblings, family and friends.

Larry is a kind, empathetic, honest and considerate young boy, but there is something that always seems to get him into trouble...he is never on time for anything! He is always late.

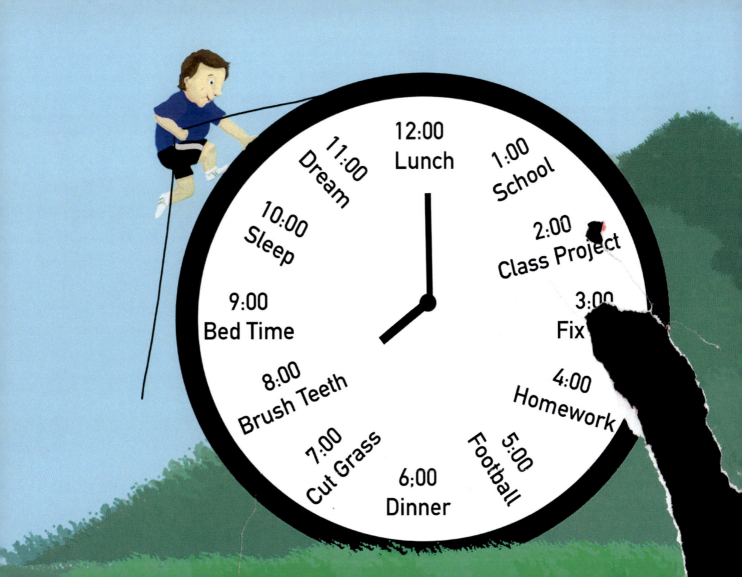

When his Dad asks him, "Larry, will you please cut the grass today?" He will do it, but it'll be dark outside by the time he gets it done.

He will help, but she is tucked into bed, fast asleep for the night by the time he gets it done.

His brother asks, "Larry, can you please fix the chain on my bike?" Larry says, "Sure, that will be easy to do."

But it is cold and snowing outside by the time he gets it done.

But practice is over by the time he gets it done.

He is the smart boy that his sisters want him to be because he always observes and learns new things along his way.

He is the strong boy that his coach wants him to be because he always stops to help strangers along his way.

He knows that it is not always important to arrive on time as long as you show up. Sometimes it is not when you get somewhere that is most important, but what you discover, who you help and what you do along the way.

The author and illustrator have known each other their entire lives. They are first cousins, friends and are now published author/illustrator for the first time together.

Made in the USA
Monee, IL
05 January 2021